I HAVE TO GROW

CASSANDRA GAISFORD

CONTENTS

Foreword	v
Praise for I Have to Grow	vii
About the Transformational Super Kids Series	xiii
About this book	1
About the Author	3
Also by The Author	5
Joy	7
Chapter 1	9
Chapter 2	11
Chapter 3	13
Chapter 4	15
Chapter 5	17
Chapter 6	19
Chapter 7	21
Chapter 8	23
Chapter 9	25
Chapter 10	27
Chapter 11	29
Chapter 12	31
Chapter 13	33
Chapter 14	35
Chapter 15	37
Epilogue	39
Please Leave a Review	43
Author's Note	45
Acknowledgments	51

EXCERPT: THE LITTLE PRINCESS

Praise for The Little Princess	57
Chapter 1	61
Chapter 2	63
Chapter 3	65
Chapter 4	67
Did you enjoy this excerpt?	69

EXCERPT: HOW TO FIND YOUR PASSION AND PURPOSE

Praise for How to Find Your Passion and Purpose	73
Author's Note	75
Introduction	79
1. Focus On Your Strengths	91
2. What Presses Your Buttons	93
3. Who Inspires You?	95
4. A Sense Of Caring Deeply	97
5. Send Your Critics Away	99
6. Persistence	101
7. Welcome to the Passion Zone!	103
Your Point of Brilliance	105
Did you enjoy this excerpt?	111
Stay In Touch	113
Copyright	117

FOREWORD

Following on from her success with *The Little Princess,* Cassandra gives us another beautiful book. Although small it holds a huge message of believing in ourselves.

So many of my clients suffer from self-doubt, stuck in their childhood messages where their light and magnificence was stunned by the words and/or actions of others, who were themselves suffering from damaging messages.

This beautiful book reminds us to believe in ourselves and while that is often too big for us to attempt, it reminds us that enlisting in the help of a trusting 'other' can be transformative. Seeking help can come in the form of a trusted friend; a focused group or a good therapist. Working on our childhood wounds allows us to step into our full power and enables us to live the life we were born to love.

~ Catherine Sloan, Intuitive Therapist

PRAISE FOR I HAVE TO GROW

"Little Hannah is my hero…

Courage is more than just standing up for yourself or doing hard things—it's doing so with compassion. Little Hannah is courageous, compassionate, talented and inspiring!

This book is the kind that can spark a transformation because the reader can see themselves within the story. I am ordering several copies for friends of various ages

~ Sheree Clark, Midlife Courage Coach

"Leads us to the best version of ourselves...

I Have to Grow is so fitting for any woman of any age. Always a good reminder to step up and become the woman we are meant to be, and always follow our Spirit for guidance as it will lead us to the best version of ourselves."

~ **Vesna Hrsto, a Naturopath and Holistic Life Coach**

"Powerful reminder in a little book...

We all need to be reminded from time to time to not let the opinions or envy from others keep us from shining brightly!"

~ **Kim**

"A great children's book...

"This was a really great book to help kids understand the impact of bullying and how it affects kids."

~ **Divya**

"Such a powerful message....

This is a splendid little book for any person aspiring to reach another level, with such a powerful message. Of never, ever listening to anyone who steals your light. Cassandra is a shining example of turning every situation, including setbacks, into learning & growing opportunities.

As one who has taken advantage of the wisdom, knowledge & ability of Cassandra, to communicate, over a number of years, I would encourage you to read this book thoroughly & think deeply on your own situation.

For her daughter Hannah, with the voice of an angel & heart of God, you have indeed been blessed."

~ Kenn Butler, CEO

DEDICATION

For my daughter Hannah Joy

who has the voice of an angel

and the heart of God.

ABOUT THE TRANSFORMATIONAL SUPER KIDS SERIES

From the bestselling author of *The Little Princess* comes a brilliant new series, *Transformational Super Kids*.

These modern-day heroes and heroines tackle modern day problems with the passion and gusto of warriors.

They defeat cruel critics, they slay savage self-esteem demons, and they show people—jealous of their kindness, talent, and beauty—that their biggest superpower is staying true to themselves.

Suitable for 'kids' of all ages. After all, aren't we all still children at heart?

ABOUT THIS BOOK

I originally wrote I Have to Grow twenty-four years ago when Hannah was four-years-old and was experiencing some very horrible bullying. When I look back, this really was my first book and heralded all those that followed with the focus on self-empowerment and overcoming shitty things that happen to good people.

Around May 20, 2019, following the galactic success of my own story of being bullied in The Little Princess, I prayed and prayed that I could find my original handwritten manuscript.

I rated my chances as slim. After all, twenty-four years is a long time to keep pieces of paper.

Thankfully, when it comes to keeping words that inspire me I'm a hoarder.

After tearing through my old filing cabinets in the garage I found it!

Thankfully, as the years since penning the original story advanced, technology upgrades and advancements in publishing have made it so easy to share my creations with the world. I've made a few minor tweaks to the hand-written story.

I hope you enjoy some of the original hand-drawings (scribbles) I have sprinkled through *I Have to Grow*. I sketched them when I first wrote the original story. Just a little bit of fun that I thought you may enjoy.

ABOUT THE AUTHOR

CASSANDRA GAISFORD is best known as *The Queen of Uplifting Inspiration.*

A former holistic therapist, award-winning artist, and #1 bestselling author. A corporate escapee, she now lives and works from her idyllic lifestyle property overlooking the Bay of Islands in New Zealand.

Cassandra's unique blend of business experience and qualifications (BCA, Dip Psych.), creative skills, and wellness and holistic training (Dip Counseling, Reiki Master Teacher) blends pragmatism and commercial savvy with rare and unique insight and out-of-the-box-thinking for anyone wanting to achieve an extraordinary life.

ALSO BY THE AUTHOR

Stories and Fairytales

The Little Princess
The Little Princess Can Fly
I Have to Grow
The Boy Who Cried

Where is Salvator Mundi?

Non-fiction Self-Empowerment Books

Mid-Life Career Rescue
How to Find Your Passion and Purpose
Bounce: Overcoming Adversity, Building Resilience and Finding Joy
Anxiety Rescue: How to Overcome Anxiety, Panic, and Stress and Reclaim Joy
Boost Your Self-Esteem and Confidence
No! Why 'No' is the New 'Yes'

and more...

More of Cassandra's practical and inspiring books on a range of life enhancing topics can be found on her website (www.cassandragaisford.com) and her author page at all good online bookstores.

Many titles are now available in audio.

I Have To grow

1

*L*ittle Hannah was happily singing on her swing when Little Angie went by.

"You think you can sing but you can't," she shouted.

Little Hannah stopped singing and ran inside.

2

"What's wrong?" Big Cassie asked as Little Hannah ran crying to her room.

"Little Angie is being mean to me," she sobbed. "She says I can't sing."

3

"*L*ittle Angie is just jealous!" Big Cassie told Little Hannah, giving her a cuddle.

"You have a beautiful voice. Promise me you'll always sing—no matter what."

4

*L*ittle Hannah snuggled into her mother's arms.

"Yes, mummy. I promise."

5

The next day Little Angie asked Little Hannah over to her house.

"Do you want to come and play hairdressers?" she asked.

"Yes, please. I'd love to," said Little Hannah, twisting her long, blonde hair around her little fingers.

6

"*D*on't be a cry baby."

Little Angie shouted as Little Hannah ran from her house, clutching the side of her head.

7

"What's wrong? Why are you holding your head?" asked Big Cassie.

"Little Angie stuck chewing gum in my hair and it wouldn't come out," Little Hannah cried.

8

"Don't worry, I'll fix it," Big Cassie said.

"Little Angie already tried," Little Hannah sobbed, reluctantly releasing her hands.

9

Big Cassie gasped in horror.

"What has she done to your hair?"

Little Hannah was totally bald on one side.

10

"Who are you?" cried Little Hannah after her mother had left the room.

"What do you mean? Isn't it obvious? I'm a Smileupagus."

11

"You look weird," Little Hannah said.

"You look weird too!" The Smileupagus said. "Why do you only have half your hair?"

"You look weird TOO!

Why do you only have half a head of hair.

12

"My friend stole the rest," Little Hannah said.

"People try and steal things from me too—my tusks for jewelry, my fur for coats, my hide for floor coverings."

13

"There are people who always try and steal from others the things they most want," the Smileupagus said.

Little Hannah stopped sobbing and listened.

"Be true to yourself, even if people criticize you or call you names, or steal from you. Don't play with those people. Play with people who love you and admire you and want you to shine."

14

"Stay away from people who make you feel small and not very nice at all," the Smileupagus said.

"Mean people always do that. Kind people make you feel wonderful."

"That sounds like something my mom, Big Cassie, would say," Little Hannah said.

15

"*B*ig Cassie always tells me that when you stand tall, you encourage others to stand tall too."

"That's good advice," the Smileupagus said.

"I have to grow, don't I?" said Little Hannah.

"Yes. You do," the Smileupagus said, as he stepped onto his flying carpet and flew away.

"You have to shine like a star."

EPILOGUE

*L*ittle Hannah looked down at the piece of paper Big Cassie had given to her that night.

On the top of the page were the words, 'I AM A STAR.'

On the bottom of the page, it said, 'GOOD THINGS ABOUT ME.'

In the middle of the page was a big star with plenty of space in it to add her own words.

Little Hannah picked up her pen and began to write.

I can sing.

I am kind.

I am loving.

I am strong...

I Have to Grow

I am a star

Good things about me.

*** THE END ***

PLEASE LEAVE A REVIEW

Word of mouth is the most powerful marketing force in the universe. If you found this book useful, I'd appreciate you rating this book and leaving a review. You don't have to say much—just a few words about how the book helped you learn something new or made you feel.

"Your books are a fantastic resource and until now I never even thought to write a review. Going forward I will be reviewing more books. So many great ones out there and I want to support the amazing people that write them."

Great reviews help people find good books.

Thank you so much! I appreciate you!

PS: If you enjoyed this book, do me a small favor to help spread the word about it and share on Facebook, Twitter and other social networks.

AUTHOR'S NOTE

This tale is based on a true story.

My daughter Hannah was born with an exceptional and innate gift which was later honed into an accomplished skill as a soprano singer.

But when my daughter was four the little girl next door told her that she couldn't sing and that she had no talent.

When the little girl next door didn't stop Hannah from singing, she tried to take something else from her. She cut Hannah's beautiful long hair.

But guess what? Her hair grew back! And so did her talent!

Hannah's talent grew and grew and grew—and it is still growing. As a teenager, she successfully auditioned for a place with Dame Malvina Major's singing academy.

"She kept her eyes shut," Hannah said enthusiastically, after her audition, "all the way through my song."

Apparently, this was a good sign.

You can learn more about Dame Malvina's passion to share her dream and help other gifted singers take their voices out to the world, here—http://www.dmmfoundation.org.nz/

Hannah decided not to pursue a career professionally as an international singer. But, as a hobby, she went on to enjoy a lot of success with her voice, including winning the lead role in a musical movie produced in Peter Jackson's studio in Wellington.

Peter Jackson is best known as the director, writer, and producer of the Lord of the Rings trilogy and the Hobbit trilogy. The fabulous New Zealand Symphony Orchestra played the background music.

Importantly, Hannah now uses her voice in the art of healing as a spiritual conduit and counselor—sending love songs to the world.

Many moons ago, Hannah and I enjoyed a magical time on the Pacific Island of Samoa. A newly married couple asked Hannah to sing and she gifted them a beautiful performance of Dame Kiri Te Kanawa's, *Ave Maria*.

A European man was sailing his large yacht and heard her voice and came to shore. "I heard the voice of an angel," he told us. I share more about this story in my travel memoir, *Four Days Out of the World* (to be released in 2019).

The European man's feedback inspired my cover.

I hope by sharing Hannah's story, you realize how important it is to share your gifts. Whether you have a talent for singing, helping others or solving puzzles —what ever it is that sparks joy within you is your gift.

You may or may not want to share it with the world but what matters most is to do what makes you happy and never ever listen to anyone who tries to steal your music.

Read to the end for an excerpt from the first book in this series—my #1 bestselling book, *The Little Princess*.

As a special thank you for reading my book I have also included an excerpt from my popular book *How to Find Your Passion and Purpose*. I've included some of my favorite chapters. Please note these aren't in the order that they appear in the book.

To learn more about the inspiration behind this book and the series please visit my blog. You may also enjoy my regular inspirational newsletters—with sneak peeks, advance reads and free giveaways.

Did you have a traumatic childhood, or know someone that did? There are so many reasons why you should look for the gift buried within your pain. If you need some help, look no further than the third book in the Transformational Super Kids series, *The Boy Who Cried*.

Available now from all good bookstores—eBook, paperback, hardback and audio!

I Have to Grow **is now available as an audiobook for your listening enjoyment.**

Check out a free sample or grab your copy from your favourite online retailer.

Check out the following written and narrated by Cassandra:

The Little Princess
The Little Princess Can Fly
I Have to Grow
The Boy Who Cried

Audio versions of these and other titles available now from all online bookstores and libraries.

ACKNOWLEDGMENTS

My daughter, Hannah—I wish for you everything that your heart desires. Without you, I would not have accomplished all the things I have in my life. You are my reason and my purpose. You are my gift. Without you, I never would have written this book!

Thank you also to my fabulous illustrator and designer Steven Novak for bringing my vision to life.

A massive thanks to my ardent supporters, including Catherine Sloan, Sheree Clark, and Kenn Butler. I truly appreciate your willingness to drop everything and read an advance copy and review.

I also want to acknowledge my mother, Joy. My mom is affectionately known as Little Joy because she is just over 5ft tall. I have written in my other books how I raised Hannah as a single mother. But in fact, I also had you.

Without your support emotionally and financially Hannah would never have blossomed into the beautiful young woman she is today. You've helped educate her, inspire her, believe in her—and me. And as I did too, you helped see her through some of her most significant mental health and relationship challenges. Thank you to the moon and back.

Francis G. Hanna, formerly of The Directions Healing Centre, your intervention in the early hours of the 11th of November 2014 was truly courageous, and I believe divinely guided.

Not only do you share the same name (almost) but you are a great healer—as Hannah herself has gone on to be. Her former partner tried to kill her—yes kill her—and you saved her life. You heard her screams for help. Where others may have cowered or turned a blind eye, you ran from your warm bed and rescued her. How amazing that a Reiki master such as you was able to help, and immediately begin to heal her trauma.

I will write more about this experience in a future

book called Saving Hannah. We desperately need more women and their families to watch out and be aware and know how to better safeguard women from the insidious and too pervasive reach of domestic violence. It is a significant problem here in New Zealand, as it globally.

To my grandmother, Molly Fairweather, I remain indebted. You taught me to crochet, and knit, and paint, and create. It is from you that I was inspired to also write love stories under my pen name Mollie Mathews. And it is from you Hannah inherited her beautiful voice and natural skill as a pianist. But more than this, despite all your years of suffering neglect, growing up as you did in a series of foster homes, you were always a shining example of joy, beauty, and grace.

Graeham William Gaisford you were an extraordinary father and grandfather. It is to you that Hannah and I owe our deep commitment to, and interest in, alternative forms of healing. Now commonly known as, and increasingly accepted by those against 'non-conventional' medicine and forms of treatment, as holistic health, you were a pioneer. I still recall you, standing in the bottom of the paddock on the farm, and telling Hannah to sing from the farmhouse so you could hear her. No easy feat—hard of hearing as you were.

Freya and Finlay Wells, my beautiful niece, and nephew thank you so much for designing the logo for my publishing company, Blue Giraffe Publishing. You were both under six-years of age at the time and already born with such great vision, wisdom, and spirit.

As Coco Chanel once said, "If you were born without wings, do nothing to prevent them from growing."

EXCERPT: THE LITTLE PRINCESS

PRAISE FOR THE LITTLE PRINCESS

"A Little Book with a Powerful Message...
An important reminder to always be true to yourself and summon the courage to follow your passions... Only *you* can live your life...GO live it!"

~ Harley

"The Little Princess is my hero...

I am a Midlife Coach, which means I help women find their moxie to do what they might not have done in the first half of their lives...I think *The Little Princess* needs to be a "required reading" text book for us all...she cuts to the heart of the lesson all of us need to hear, over and over again. *The Little Princess* embodies courage. She is my hero."

~ Sheree Clark, Midlife Courage Coach

***The Little Princess* is 'brilliant…**
Short concise & full of tremendous vision & wisdom, expressed lovingly. Many of the comments read true for my own journey. I recognize my passion to be different than many others, my persistence to succeed, & the pure joy I have at the end of each day when I lay down my head & give thanks."

~ Kenn Butler, CEO

"Very uplifting and inspiring…
I love everything Cassandra writes, the queen of uplifting inspiration! This is a little book, the story basically teaches you to have faith in your dreams, stand firm and don't let others rain on your parade.. We are all searching for purpose and passion, everybody hurts and sometimes we find ourselves on the receiving end of somebody else's insecurities, when they project their anger, jealousy etc onto us..

The old woman who puts the little princess down is really just jealous and stuck in her own life."

~ Reviewer UK

"A reminder of the truth in all of us...
The Little Princess is a great short story as a reminder of the truth in all of us; Don't judge, take loving kindness as a guideline in life, but stay true to yourself; A powerful message! Like all the books by this author, it is a guideline to live a wise life."

~ Maartje Jager, Designer

1

*O*nce upon a time there was a young woman who wanted to make a difference in the world.

She wanted to help others. She wanted to help people overcome depression, anxiety, and feeling sad.

She wanted to to help them feel inspired, joyful and happy.

She just wasn't sure how.

2

*O*ne day she had an inspired idea. "I can help people find their passion and purpose," she thought.

Her heart fluttered then soared higher and higher and higher—far, far, far away.

Almost beyond the reach of her doubts and fears.

3

*S*he felt so excited—but also scared. She decided to feel the fear and create something anyway.

She knew people often struggled to find the time to read, and she wanted to make it easy and fun for people to find inspiration and help.

She decided to design a pack of inspirational cards that would enable people to help themselves and become empowered to transform their lives.

The cards would give people ideas, encourage them to dream, and give them hope.

4

She thought about the angel cards that had given her so much relief when she was an anxious child.

"Wouldn't it be fun to create something similar?" she thought.

Each card would have an inspirational quote on one side and a self-help strategy on the other.

DID YOU ENJOY THIS EXCERPT?

Grab your own copy of *The Little Princess*

Follow your heart! Heed the call for courage.

Feeling stuck, depressed or demotivated? There are so many reasons why you should follow your dreams. If you need some motivation, look no further than this book.

Part moral allegory and part spiritual autobiography, *The Little Princess* is a timeless charm which tells the story of a young woman who leaves the safety of fitting in with everyone else, to follow her heart.

Be inspired by this journey to transformation and

self-acceptance, and self-belief as she learns to overcome the vagaries of adult behavior. Her personal odyssey culminates in a voyage of self-belief, passion, and purpose.

From the best-selling author of Mid-Life Career Rescue, Stress Less and How to Find Your Passion and Purpose: a powerful, inspiring, and practical book about boosting resilience, overcoming obstacles and moving forward after life's inevitable setbacks.

Find out what strategies are sabotaging your success. Find and follow your passion and purpose faster.

The Little Princess is available in eBook, paperback, hardback and audiobook from all great online retailers.

Be the first to know when other books in the Transformational Super Kids series and the audio version is released!

You'll find details in the Stay in Touch section to follow.

EXCERPT: HOW TO FIND YOUR PASSION AND PURPOSE

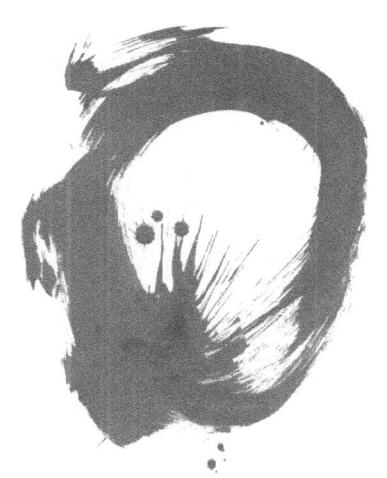

**PRAISE FOR HOW TO FIND YOUR
PASSION AND PURPOSE**

"This little book on a BIG topic that resonates with me packs a lot of wisdom that is worth investing time in. Cassandra challenges us to "Dare to Dream!" Take the time and make the effort to find the work you feel passionate about; You could read this in less than two hours and be on your way to sculpting out a new way of living if you're not living your passionate lifestyle yet."

**~ Scott.B. Allan, Author of #1
bestseller *Empower Your Thoughts***

"This excellent little book is quick to read but left me with much to think about and many practical steps to take to find my passion and incorporate it into my life. There are several free resources to download which increase the worth of this already very valuable book."

~ Jenny Cliff, Author of *The Music Inside*

"*How to Find Your Passion and Purpose* is a positive and enabling companion and offers much. It encourages us to identify our passion and interests, to live from our core values and use our signature strengths creatively. It highlights that it's never too late to make changes, to get on the path of true fulfillment and make a living. Dig into this book and let Cassandra be your guide, inspiration and coach as she calls forth your creativity and gives practical steps to take you where you need to go next. Step into this ride joyfully and create your future."

~ Jasbindar Singh, Business Psychologist and Author of *Get Your Groove Back*

AUTHOR'S NOTE

This book is a concise guide to making the most of your life. It began its journey some years ago as *The Passion Pack* – a set of 40 cards created to help people live and work with passion.

The vision was simple: a few short, easy to digest tips for time-challenged people who were looking for inspiration and practical strategies to encourage positive change.

From my own experience, I knew that people didn't need a large wad of words to feel inspired, gain clarity and be stimulated to take action.

In coaching and counselling sessions I'd encourage my clients to ask a question they would like answered. The questions could be specific, such as, 'How can I make a living from my passion?' Or vague, for example, 'What do I most need to know?'

Then I'd ask them to pick a card at random. Without fail, they were astounded by the card's potent relevance. Disbelieving eyes widened in astonishment as they read either the quote or the main message they received. Many would say, "These cards are magic."

Orders flooded in from global recruitment consultancies, primary schools, colleges, universities, not-for-profit organizations, financial institutions and other multi-national commercial entities. I was asked to speak at conferences around the world about the power of passion. It was amazing to see how popular and successful *The Passion Pack* became, transcending age, gender, and socio-economic differences.

In this era of information obesity the need for simple, life-affirming messages is even more important. If you are looking for inspiration and practical tips, in short, sweet sound bites, this guide is for you.

Similarly, if you are a grazer, or someone more methodical, this guide will also work for you. Pick a page at random, or work through the steps sequentially. I encourage you to experiment, be open-minded and try new things. I promise you will achieve outstanding results.

Clive, a 62-year-old man who had suffered work-related burnout, did! He thought that creating a passion journal, *Tip 10* in this guide, was childish – something other stressed executives in his men's support group would balk at. But once he'd taken up the challenge he told me enthusiastically,

"They loved it!" They are using their passion journals to visualize, gain clarity, and create their preferred futures. Clive is using it to help manifest his new purpose-driven coaching business.

Let experience be your guide. Give your brain a well-needed break. Let go of 'why', and embrace how you *feel*, or how you want to feel. Honor the messages from your intuition and follow your path with heart.

Laura, who at one stage seemed rudderless career-wise, did just that. She was guided to *Tip 14: Who Inspires You?* Following that, her motivation to live and work like those she looked up to sparked a determination to start her own business. It was that simple.

At the time of writing I've just turned to Tip *31: Fear Of Success*. It's a timely reminder of just how far following my passion has taken me – the shy girl who was once afraid of being seen. The quote is as apt for me as I feel it may be for you:

"Your playing small doesn't serve the world."

Here's to living with passion and purpose!

INTRODUCTION

> **"Mary Oliver says in one of her poems, 'Tell me, what is it that you plan to do with your one wild and precious life?' Me, I intend to live passionately."**
> Isabel Allende, Novelist

Finding a job you want and living a life you love is impossible without passion, enthusiasm, zest, inspiration and the deep satisfaction that comes from doing something that delivers you some kind of buzz.

Yet, it's staggeringly, and dishearteningly, true that many people don't know what they are passionate about, or how they can turn it into a rewarding career. Some research suggests that only 10% of people are living and working with passion. Hence my passion for passion and helping create more positive change in the world.

If you're like many people who don't know what they are passionate about or what gives your life meaning and purpose, this book will help provide the answers.

If you have been told it's not realistic to work and live with passion, this book will help change your mindset.

Together we'll help you get your mojo back, challenge your current beliefs and increase your sense of possibility. By tapping into a combination of practical career strategies, Law of Attraction principles, and the spiritual powers of manifestation, you'll reawaken dreams, boost your self-awareness, empower your life and challenge what you thought was possible.

We'll do this in an inspired yet structured way by strengthening your creative thinking skills, boosting your self-awareness and helping you identify your non-negotiable ingredients for career success and happiness. Little steps will lead naturally to bigger leaps, giving you the courage and confidence to follow your passion and fly free towards career happiness and life fulfillment.

What you're about to read isn't another self-help book; it's a self-empowerment book. It offers ways to increase your self-knowledge. From that knowledge comes the power to create a life worth living.

How to Find Your Passion and Purpose will help you:

- Explore and clarify your passions, interests, and life purpose
- Build a strong foundation for happiness and success
- Value your gifts, and talents and confirm your work-related strengths
- Direct your energies positively toward your preferred future
- Strengthen your creative thinking skills, and ability to identify possible roles you would enjoy, including self-employment
- Have the courage to follow your dreams and super-charge the confidence needed to make an inspired change
- Find your point of brilliance

Let's look briefly at what each chapter in this book will cover:

Step One, "The Call For Passion" will help you explore the meaning of passion and discover the benefits of following it, and consequences of ignoring your passion. You'll identify any passion blocking beliefs and intensify passion-building beliefs to boost your chances of success.

Step Two, "Discover Your Passion," will help you to identify your own sources of passion and passion criteria. What you'll discover may be a complete surprise and open up a realm of opportunities you've never considered.

Step Three, "Passion at Work," will assist you in identifying career options and exploring ways to develop your career in light of your passions and life purpose.

Step Four, "Live Your Passion," looks at passion beyond the world of work and ways to achieve greater balance and fulfillment. You'll also identify strategies to overcome obstacles and to maximize your success.

How to Find Your Passion and Purpose concludes

with showing you how to identify your point of brilliance.

How To Use This Book—Your Virtual Coach

To really benefit from this book think of it as your 'virtual' coach—answer the questions and complete the additional exercises that you'll find in the chapters and free extras.

Questions are great thought provokers. Your answers to these questions will help you gently challenge current assumptions and gain greater clarity about your goals and desires.

All the strategies are designed to facilitate greater insight and to help you integrate new learnings. Resist the urge to just process information in your head. We learn best by doing. Research has repeatedly proven that the act of writing deepens your knowledge and understanding.

For example, a study conducted by Dr. David K. Pugalee, found that journal writing was an effective instructional tool and aided learning. His research found that writing helped people organize and describe internal thoughts and thus improve their problem solving-skills.

Henriette Klauser, Ph.D., also provides compelling evidence in her book, *Write It Down and Make It Happen*, that writing helps you clarify what you want and enables you to make it happen.

Writing down your insights is the area where people like motivational guru Tony Robbins, say that the winners part from the losers, because the losers always find a reason not to write things down. Harsh but perhaps true!

Keeping A Passion Journal

A passion journal is also a great place to store sources of inspiration to support you through the career planning and change process. For some tips to help you create your own inspirational passion journal, go to the media page on my website and watch my television interview and interview with other experts here:

http://www.cassandragaisford.com/media

This Book Is Magical

This book proves less really is more. Sometimes all it takes to radically transform your life is one word, one sentence, one powerful but simple strategy to ignite inspiration and reawaken a sense of possibility.

I have successfully used the knowledge I'm sharing with you in this book professionally with my clients and personally during numerous reinventions.

I stand by every one of the 4 steps and the 40+ strategies you will learn here, not just because they are grounded in strong evidence-based, scientific and spiritual principles, but also because I have successfully used them to create turnaround, after turnaround in nearly every area of my life.

How to Find Your Passion and Purpose is the culmination of all that I have experienced and all that I have learned, applied and taught others for over two decades. I don't practice what I preach; I preach what I have practiced—because it gets results.

Why Did I Write This Book?

If you are curious about *The Passion Pack* and why I created *How To Find Your Passion and Purpose*, you may like to check out my blog post here:

http://www.cassandragaisford.com/2557-2/

Setting You Up For Success

"Aren't you setting people up for failure?" a disillusioned career coach once challenged me.

Twenty-five years of cumulative professional experience as a career coach and counselor, helping people work with passion and still pay the bills, answers that question. I'm setting people up for success. I'm not saying it will happen instantly, but if you follow the advice in this book, it will happen. I promise.

I've proven repeatedly, both personally and professionally, that thinking differently and creatively, rationally and practically, while also harnessing the power of your heart, and applying the principles of manifestation, really works. In this book, I'll show you why—and how.

A large part of my philosophy and the reason behind my success with clients is my fervent belief that to achieve anything worthy of life you need to follow your passion. And I'm in good company.

As media giant Oprah Winfrey once said, "Passion is

energy. Feel the power that comes from focusing on what excites you."

Passion's Pay Cheque

By discovering your passion and purpose you will tap into a huge source of potential energy and prosperity. Pursuing your passion can be profitable on many levels:

- When you do what you love, your true talent will reveal itself; passion can't be faked
- You'll be more enthusiastic about your pursuits
- You'll have more energy to overcome obstacles
- You will be more determined to make things happen
- You will enjoy your work
- Your work will become a vehicle for self-expression
- Passion will give you a competitive edge
- You'll enjoy your life and magnetize positive experiences toward you

Without passion, you don't have energy, and without energy you have nothing.

You have to let love, desire, and passion, not fear or ambivalence or apathy, propel you forward. Yet worryingly, research suggests that less than 10% of people are following their passion. Perhaps that's why there is so much unhappiness in the world.

Don't waste another day feeling uninspired. Don't be the person who spends a life of regret, or waits until they retire before they follow their passions, be you. Don't be the person too afraid to make a change for the better, or who wishes they could lead a significant life. Make the change now. Before it's too late.

Extra Support: Companion Workbook

How to Find Your Passion and Purpose (the book) offers you information about overcoming adversity, building resilience and finding joy. Reading a book is great but applying the teachings and writing things down in a dedicated space helps bring the learning alive, deepens your self awareness, and enables you to make real world change. Reading gives you knowledge, but reflecting upon and applying that knowledge creates true empowerment.

By writing and recording your responses you're rewriting the story of your life. As Seth Godin states, "Here's the thing: The book that will most change your life is the book you write. The act of writing things down, of justifying your actions, of being cogent and clear, and forthright—that's how you change."

The *How to Find Your Passion and Purpose Companion Workbook* will support you through the learning and show you how to create real and meaningful change in your life...simply and joyfully.

Reach For Your Dreams

Passion, happiness, joy, fulfillment, love—call it what you will, my deepest desire is that this book encourages you to reach for your dreams, to never settle, to believe in the highest aspirations you have for yourself.

You have so many gifts, so many talents that the world so desperately needs. We need people like you who care about what they do, who want to live and work with passion and purpose.

I promise that if you follow the steps in this book you'll discover what you really want to do, clarify what you can do, and create powerful but simple strategies to make your dream a reality. You'll find a job that you love, one that adds more joy to your life and gives you a sense of meaning, purpose, and fulfillment.

And what I can promise you is this—whatever your circumstances, it's never too late to re-create yourself and your life. So, what are you waiting for?

Let's get started!

1
FOCUS ON YOUR STRENGTHS

"Where talent and interest intersect expect a masterpiece."
John Ruskin, Painter

We often take our 'natural knacks' or gifts for granted. However, the skills that are easiest for us can provide a good clue to areas we are most passionate about. Sometimes others have a greater awareness of our strengths and areas of passion than we do!

What skills and talents come most naturally to you?

What strengths do others notice and admire?
What are the other skills and strengths that give you a buzz?

WRITE these insights in your passion journal. Add to it and review it regularly.

PASSION FLOWS, it can't be forced. Don't underestimate the things that come easiest for you.

2
WHAT PRESSES YOUR BUTTONS

"The world often continues to allow evil because it isn't angry enough."
Bede Jarrett, Writer

*P*assionate anger, constructively used, could become the fuel that drives you, the fuel that drives your passion.

WHAT PRESSES YOUR BUTTONS? It may be specific things going on in your life now or wider issues about life in general, such as injustice, racism etc. Gain greater awareness by exploring why your buttons are being pushed.

ARE there any ways you could you use your anger to benefit others and bring about positive change?

3
WHO INSPIRES YOU?

"Inspiring people are like vitamins for our souls."
Sark, Writer

Who or what inspires you? Think about the sorts of books and magazines you love to read, or people and things you love to be around. What about them is interesting to you?

Look for your heroes and allow others' enthusiasm and passion to excite you! Play detective. Do some research, go and talk to people who are passionate about some aspect of their life, read books about inspiring people or themes that really capture your imagination.

WHAT COULD you do to get more inspired?

4
A SENSE OF CARING DEEPLY

"To succeed you have to believe in something with such a passion that it becomes a reality."
Anita Roddick, Businesswoman

Real passion is more than a fad or fleeting enthusiasm. It can't be turned on and off like a tap. It's a full-bodied belief or commitment to something.

WHAT DO you care deeply about? Discovering all the

things that you feel strongly about is not always easy. Look for some clues to your beliefs by catching the times you use words such as "should" or "must."

What do you really believe in? It might be honesty, openness, freedom, equality, or justice. Record your insights in your passion journal.

5
SEND YOUR CRITICS AWAY

"Keep away from people who try to belittle your ambitions. Small people always do that, but the really great make you feel that you, too, can become great."
Mark Twain, Writer

If you are steering towards having more passion in your life, people may be jealous or threatened and criticize you. Be passionate anyway!

Don't be put off by negative feedback. Don't wait for

others to give approval to your life. Send your critics on a holiday.

Be brave. Be bold. Be firm. Be audacious. You'll soon conquer your fears and convince others.

Who could you look to for inspiration, encouragement, and support?

Check out my 2019 release The Little Princess to learn how I sent my critics away!

6
PERSISTENCE

> "Obstacles don't have to stop you. If you run into a wall, don't turn around and give up. Figure out how to climb it, go through it, or work around it."
> Michael Jordan, Basketball Legend

*T*hings worth having in life don't always come easily. You have to want something with such a passion that you're willing to persevere in the face of setbacks.

Every time you persist in the face of obstacles your

belief in yourself will sky rocket until it reaches the point where you become unstoppable!

How PERSISTENT ARE YOU? Do you give up easily? How can you keep yourself motivated to put in the time and energy it may take to move ahead and reach your goals?

WELCOME TO THE PASSION ZONE!

> **"If you follow your bliss, doors will open for you that wouldn't have opened for anyone else."**
> Joseph Campbell, Writer

*Y*ou've made it! By reading and applying the practical strategies in this book you've taken the first step to leading a happier and more fulfilled life.

Well done! But remember, you're not there yet. Being passionate is an ongoing commitment that takes time and effort. But just imagine how great you'll feel when you're living your passion.

Keep this book handy and refer to it regularly. It will help you achieve your goals and keep your passion alive. Enlist the support of a career or life coach if you need more help or motivation to reach your goals.

You've completed a tremendous journey. Thank you for allowing me to travel with you.

Before we part company you may find it helpful to summarize all that you have learned by clarifying your passion point or point of brilliance.

YOUR POINT OF BRILLIANCE

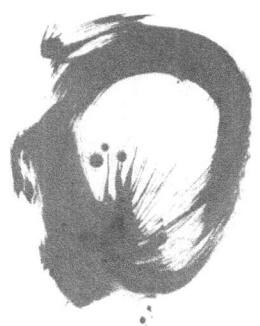

Your point of brilliance is where you truly shine. It's your point of passion. It's the intersection of your favorite gifts, and talents, your deepest interests and enthusiasms, and all that motivates, inspires and drives you.

It's the place of fire and alchemy, magnetizing and attracting people, situations and opportunities to you.

But you must show up. You must commit to being authentically you. And you must stand in your own truth. You know what makes you bloom and what makes you wither. You know when you're opening and when you're closing.

Be deliberate and focused in the pursuit of your happiness. Target your intentions on your dreams and desires, and ensure your choices align with what makes you happy.

Get real about your motives. Why do you want to reach your goals? Are your following your path with heart, your life purpose, your true destiny? If you follow your chosen path, will you reach your place of true bliss and authentic happiness?

Are you grounded in your truth, or are you chasing someone else's goals, or the lure of fantasy and ego?

Remember the perfect career and life for you is one that:

- You're passionate about

- Interests you
- Fills you with purpose
- Aligns with your highest values
- Utilizes your favorite talents
- Allows you to express yourself
- Fulfills your potential
- Facilitates your growth
- Feeds your mind, body and soul
- Boosts self-esteem and confidence
- Makes you happy
- Fuels your energy
- Gives life
- Enables your goals
- Is your point of brilliance

These are not unrealistic expectations. Target your intentions, and shoot straight for the stars. Don't settle for anything less.

You may find it helpful to summarize the insights you've gained from reading this book. The following exercise can also help you stay on track.

Your Passion Point is your Point of Brilliance

I've always loved John Ruskin's quote, "Where talent, interest and motivation intersect expect a masterpiece."

Using this as your guide, you may like to draw three circles. List your areas of motivation in one (passion, purpose, values, goals etc.); Your interests and obsessions in another; Your favorite skills and talents in the third.

Note where they overlap. This is your internal world, and what I call your Passion Point, or Point of Brilliance.

Surround these three circles with a fourth to enclose them. They symbolize the external world—both the practical earth and the higher heavens.

How Can Your Point Of Brilliance Serve?

To generate more career options, knowing what will be needed or in demand, now and in the future, can yield gold. What needs can you fulfill when you're aligned with your Passion Point? What economic, demographic, social, environmental or other needs can you serve? This is the work you are called to do and where you will truly shine.

It doesn't need to have a massive job title, or be about saving the world. But whatever you chose to do has to fulfill a need. Economics 101—no need, no demand. Of course, if money is no barrier, you are freer to pursue your own needs without this added focus. By doing this you may just create a demand, or make the world a happier place. Importantly, you'll be happy.

Balance The Law of Intention with The Law of Detachment

Remember to balance the Law of Intention with The Law of Detachment. Nothing you want is upstream. Resist the urge to panic, if things don't happen as quickly as you'd like. Go with the flow.

Trust. Cultivate faith. Believe. Allow no doubt.

You may think the outcome has to happen in a certain way, on a certain day, to reach your goal. But human willpower cannot make everything happen. Spirit has its own idea, of how the arrow flies, and upon what wind it travels.

It may not happen overnight, but if you maintain

your focus, and take inspired action, and follow your heart, your time will come.

I promise!

If, because of some strange twist of fate it doesn't? At least you tried. A life of no regrets - now that's worth striving for.

> **"Listen to your gut but sometimes do it anyway. Playing safe is easy but boring."**
>
> Katie Couric, Yahoo Global News Anchor and Cancer Awareness Campaigner

DID YOU ENJOY THIS EXCERPT?

If you need more help to find and live your life purpose you can read my book, *How to Find Your Passion and Purpose: Four Easy Steps to Discover a Job You Want and Live the Life You Love* will help—available as a paperback and eBook and audiobook from all good online bookstores. I'm so excited to let you know that it will soon be available as an audio book—narrated by me!

Or you may prefer to take my online course, and watch inspirational and practical videos and other strategies to help you to fulfill your potential—https://the-coaching-lab.teachable.com/p/follow-your-passion-and-purpose-to-prosperity

If you need more help to create a passion and purpose inspired business, *The Passion-Driven Business Planning Journal:The Effortless Path to Manifesting Your Business and Career Goals*, available as a paperback and eBook will help. Available from all good online bookstores.

STAY IN TOUCH

Become a fan and Continue To Be Supported, Encouraged, and Inspired

Subscribe to my newsletter and follow me on BookBub (https://www.bookbub.com/profile/cassandra-gaisford) and be the first to know about my new releases and giveaways

www.cassandragaisford.com
www.facebook.com/cassandra.gaisford
www.instagram.com/cassandragaisford
www.youtube.com/cassandragaisfordnz
www.pinterest.com/cassandraNZ
www.linkedin.com/in/cassandragaisford
www.twitter.com/cassandraNZ

BLOG

Subscribe and be inspired by regular posts to help you increase your wellness, follow your bliss, slay self-doubt, and sustain healthy habits.

Learn more about how to achieve happiness and success at work and life by visiting my blog:

www.cassandragaisford.com/archives

SPEAKING EVENTS

Cassandra is available internationally for speaking events aimed at wellness strategies, motivation, inspiration and as a keynote speaker.

She has an enthusiastic, humorous and passionate style of delivery and is celebrated for her ability to motivate, inspire and enlighten.

For information navigate to www.cassandragaisford.com/contact/speaking

To ask Cassandra to come and speak at your workplace or conference, contact: cassandra@cassandragaisford.com

NEWSLETTERS

For inspiring tools and helpful tips subscribe to Cassandra's free newsletters here: http://www.cassandragaisford.com

Sign up now and receive a free eBook to help you find your passion and purpose!
http://eepurl.com/bEArfT

COPYRIGHT

Copyright © 2019 Cassandra Gaisford
Published by Blue Giraffe Publishing 2019

Blue Giraffe Publishing is a division of Worklife Solutions Ltd.

Cover Design by Steven Novak

All rights reserved. No part of this publication may be reproduced, distributed, or transmitted in any form or by any means, including photocopying, recording, or other electronic or mechanical methods, without the prior written permission of the author or publisher, except in the case of brief quotations embodied in reviews and certain other non-commercial uses permitted by copyright law.

Neither the publisher nor the author are engaged in rendering professional advice or services to the individual reader. The ideas, procedures, and suggestions contained in this book are not intended as a substitute for psychotherapy, counseling, or consulting with your physician.

The intent of the author is only to offer information of a general nature to help you in your quest for emotional, physical, and spiritual well-being.

Any use of information in this book is at the reader's discretion and risk. Neither the author nor the publisher can be held responsible for any loss, claim or damage arising out of the use, or misuse, of the suggestions made, the failure to take medical advice or for any material on third party websites.

ISBN PRINT: 978-1-0706000-5-5 (Amazon)

ISBN PRINT: 978-0-9951289-7-2 (wide)

ISBN EBOOK: 978-0-9951138-5-5

ISBN HARDCOVER: 978-0-9951138-9-3

First Edition

www.ingramcontent.com/pod-product-compliance
Lightning Source LLC
Chambersburg PA
CBHW020258030426
42336CB00010B/825